D0824918

A
PRACTICAL GUIDE
TO
GOVERNING YOUR
VOLUNTEER
ORGANIZATION

How to provide your not-for-profit organization
with effective leadership and sound stewardship

TOM ABBOTT
Association Management Consultants Inc.

Note for Librarians: A cataloguing record for this book is available from Library and Archives Canada at www.collectionscanada.ca/amicus/index-e.html
ISBN 1-4120-7595-5

Printed in Victoria, BC, Canada. Printed on paper with minimum 30% recycled fibre. Trafford's print shop runs on "green energy" from solar, wind and other environmentally-friendly power sources.

TRAFFORD
PUBLISHING™

Offices in Canada, USA, Ireland and UK
This book was published *on-demand* in cooperation with Trafford Publishing. On-demand publishing is a unique process and service of making a book available for retail sale to the public taking advantage of on-demand manufacturing and Internet marketing. On-demand publishing includes promotions, retail sales, manufacturing, order fulfilment, accounting and collecting royalties on behalf of the author.

Book sales for North America and international:
Trafford Publishing, 6E–2333 Government St.,
Victoria, BC v8t 4p4 CANADA
phone 250 383 6864 (toll-free 1 888 232 4444)
fax 250 383 6804; email to orders@trafford.com
Book sales in Europe:
Trafford Publishing (uk) Limited, 9 Park End Street, 2nd Floor
Oxford, UK oxi ihh UNITED KINGDOM
phone 44 (0)1865 722 113 (local rate 0845 230 9601)
facsimile 44 (0)1865 722 868; info.uk@trafford.com
Order online at:
trafford.com/05-2490

10 9 8 7 6 5 4 3

For Joan Abbott
and
Tom Abbott Jr.

TABLE OF CONTENTS

CHAPTER ONE

YOUR ROLE
AS A DIRECTOR

YOUR ROLE AS A DIRECTOR

Whether you are already "working" as a volunteer director in a not-for-profit organization (NPO) or have just joined the Board of Directors—congratulations! You are one of the many hundreds of thousands of people who step forward each year to help organizations on a volunteer basis. Thanks to your dedication and hard work, your members, stakeholders, and communities enjoy improved benefits, opportunities, and services. In the case of organizations that do charitable work, volunteers have created a society that is more caring and committed to helping those in need—in this country and around the world.

Purpose of This Book

The purpose of this book is to provide a short, self-contained guide for NPO success—a book of significant value to volunteer directors who serve on the organization's board. It will also be of benefit to the chief executive officer (CEO) and staff members of the NPO.

This book is intended to be useful to a wide spectrum of NPOs. In particular it is addressed to directors of small to mid-sized organizations, including associations, charities, and public sector groups. The material dealing with planning, governance, board training, and monitoring will also be of benefit to larger NPOs.

Terminology

For ease of reference in this book, the term *organization* will generally be used to mean the NPO or charity. The word *association* is used in some places where this better indicates the organization being discussed. The term *CEO* or *Chief Executive Officer* means the senior staff officer responsible to the board for overall management of the organization (common alternative titles being Executive Director or President). The Board of Directors will generally be abbreviated to *board*, and the Chair of the Board (the senior elected officer who presides at board meetings) will be referred to as the *board chair* or simply *chair*. These and other terms used in the book are defined in Exhibit 1.1 at the end of this chapter.

Governing for the Future

There are over 160,000 not-for-profit organizations in Canada and over 2 million in the United States. Not all of these NPOs succeed in their goals. Some do not even survive beyond a year or two of operation.

In order to be successful, NPOs require structure, direction, resources and accountability. The structure includes clearly defined roles for the board, the board chair, the CEO and staff, and the all-important committees and task forces of the organization. Together, these aspects are often termed the governance model (see Chapter 7). It must be clear who is responsible for planning, policy setting, implementing plans and policies, monitoring performance, funding, running effective meetings, and communicating to the membership, as well as how each of these processes will work.

Let us start with your legal responsibilities as a director, then go on to define your dual role.

Legal Responsibilities

Serving on a volunteer board is full of challenges; and it is not without risks. It surprises some volunteer directors to learn that their legal responsibilities are virtually identical to corporate directors, even though volunteer directors largely contribute their time, energy, and talents without remuneration.

In most jurisdictions, the law requires that directors of volunteer boards:

- Act honestly, in good faith, and in the best interests of the organization.

- Exercise the care, diligence, and skill of a reasonably prudent person in exercising their powers and performing their functions as directors.

Well, how can you do that? What is your role in providing sound stewardship and effective leadership to your organization?

Your Dual Role as a Director

You have two fundamental and concurrent roles. On behalf of the members and/or stakeholders of your organization, your dual role, in cooperation with other board members, is the following:

- **Leadership:** To decide where the organization should be going now and in the future

- **Stewardship:** To ensure that as it moves forward, the organization's assets are as sound (or better) at the end of your term on the board as they were when you arrived (that means not only financial assets, but also reputation in the community and society).

You should be equally clear about the kind of activity that is not part of your role. Your role as a member of the board does not include such operational activities as these:

- Assisting the executive director to hire staff, decide on salaries,or discipline employees
- Writing or publishing your organization's newsletter
- Organizing membership golf tournaments or other social events
- Deciding on the best computer system for the organization's office
- Deciding on the type of the carpets, telephones, drapes or anything else in the office.

These activities are all at the level of detailed implementation, which is not the governance level at which you should operate as a director.

Many directors give too much attention to the detailed tasks and pay too little attention to their true roles of leadership and stewardship. Each of the chapters in this book will help you spend your valuable time as a volunteer board member doing the right governance tasks better—leaving the detailed work to those in the organization whose job is concerned with implementing the direction given by the board.

What You Will Find in This Book

This book comprises ten largely self-contained chapters. The first six chapters provide guidance on the work of the organization from planning and policy making through to implementation and then to monitoring performance. Chapter 2 deals with planning, including an overview of strategic planning and how it gets done; also, this chapter covers the development of the Mission Statement, goals, and objectives and how they inter-relate. Chapter 3 addresses the role of the board and CEO in policy setting at the board and staff (administrative) levels respectively.

In Chapter 4, the focus changes from the job of developing plans and policies to the job of implementing plans and policies. This theme of "how things get done" is expanded in Chapter 5 on the working of board committees and task forces. Chapter 6 deals with the critical governance task of monitoring the performance of the organization in relation to the approved plans and policies.

> *Despite their almost limitless diversity, nonprofits are also alike in that in many—maybe a majority— (their) governance structure malfunctions as often as it functions...*[1] –Peter Drucker
>
> *... most of what the majority of boards do either does not need to be done or is a waste of time when done by the board.*[2] – John Carver

The last four chapters address the special issues of governance models, training and orientation, financial stewardship, and meeting success factors. Chapter 7 takes a broad look at three alternative models of governance— each of which is designed to get the job done, but which assign different functions to the board and the CEO and staff. This issue of "Who does what, and with how much authority?" needs much attention and consensus before the NPO is ready for the essential task of training board directors. Chapter 8 addresses training issues, including what to cover in board orientation sessions.

Chapter 9 on financial stewardship provides an overview of funding issues, including cost containment initiatives, revenue maximization through dues and non-dues revenues, the Membership Value Proposition, financial controls, and the concepts of implications of generating healthy surpluses on activities and programs. Finally, Chapter 10 addresses the importance of meetings in the work of an NPO and how board directors can make the most of their time on committees and task forces; this chapter includes ten simple rules for successful meetings, a sample agenda, and a reference table for the most essential motions and votes.

---

[1] Peter Drucker, *Managing for the Future: The 1990s and Beyond,* (New York: Truman Talley Books/Dutton), 219.

[2] John Carver, *Boards That Make A Difference: A New Design for Leadership in Non-Profit and Public Organizations,* 1st ed. (San Francisco: Jossey-Bass), 1990, xiii.

There was one clear focus in writing this book: to create a small, readable book that would be used by volunteer boards and staff to help them do a better job on behalf of their clients, members, and stakeholders. Much of the material here has been tried, tested, and implemented in successful organizations across the not-for-profit sector in Canada and the United States. The guidance in this book will make your work in the organization more productive and satisfying, and help you contribute to the long-term success of your NPO.

Exhibit 1.1 COMMON NPO TERMINOLOGY	
Not-for-profit organization (NPO)	An organization governed by a volunteer Board of Directors, with no shareholders, for which the generation of profit is not the prime objective. May also be called (in the U.S.) a nonprofit organization. In general usage, the terms not-for-profit organization, association, society, and charity are often used interchangeably though this is not technically correct.
Charity	An organization governed by a volunteer board and established for charitable purposes as defined by legislation.
Mission Statement	A clear, concise, and inspiring statement that specifies the purpose and direction of the organization, what it does, for whom, and where.
Goals	What is intended to be accomplished to achieve the mission.
Objectives	Specifically how the goals are to be reached.
Constitution	A short document stating the name of the organization and its general purposes. The original constitution and changes to it must be approved by the membership and the government.
Bylaws	A longer document that outlines the general operational rules of the organization; for example, categories of membership, rules for member meetings including the annual general meeting (AGM), rules for board meetings, general duties of officers and directors. The original bylaws and changes to the bylaws must be approved by the membership and filed with the government.
Membership	The group from whom all power and authority in the association flows.
Board	The group to whom the membership grants powers to act on its behalf. May be called Board of Governors or Board of Directors or Council.

Chair	The individual who presides at meetings of the board as the senior elected officer.
Chief Executive Officer (CEO)	The senior staff officer who has overall management responsibility for an organization. The CEO is appointed by and reports directly to the Board of Directors. The CEO hires and manages other staff in order to implement the policies and programs approved by the board. In some organizations this person may be called the Executive Director.
Board Committee	An ongoing committee established by the board and reporting to it. Sometimes referred to as a board statutory committee. It frequently deals with responsibilities outlined in the bylaws or enabling legislation of the organization, for example, the Nominations Committee, Audit Committee, or Discipline/ Ethics Committee.
Policy Task Force	A special type of committee established by the board, allocated a specific task dealing with a policy issue and reporting to the board within a specific timeframe; for example, Governance Task Force, Membership Classification Task Force, or Unification Task Force.
CEO Committee	A committee established by and reporting to the CEO. Sometimes called a CEO working committee. It deals with operational or management matters such as publishing and distributing the organization's newsletter, putting on the organization's annual conference, or maintaining computer systems.
Advisory Council	Group of respected volunteers called upon from time to time to offer advice to the board. Sometimes comprised of past presidents.
The Membership Value Proposition (MVP)	The value received (tangible and intangible) from belonging to the association must be equal to or greater than the cost of belonging to the association.

Two other terms you will see in the literature of organizations (see Chapter 2):

Vision Statement	A simple and concise picture of an ideal, desired future for the organization.
Values Statement	A clear and concise statement of how the organization should act in order to reach its vision.

CHAPTER TWO

PLANNING

PLANNING

One of the most significant differences between for-profit and not-for-profit organizations is that for the NPO, the "bottom line" is not a single number against which to measure the success of the organization. The NPO does not measure its success in terms of generated profits, but rather in terms of the accomplishment of other non-financial goals and objectives.

That is precisely why establishing the organization's plan and monitoring the implementation of the plan is so important for not-for-profit organizations.

By planning in this context, we really mean strategic planning, and that is the function of the board. In fact, we could say that the board "owns" the Strategic Plan on behalf of the members. It represents a higher level of planning than the detailed (usually annual) Operational Plan that is prepared by the CEO and staff after the board approves the Strategic Plan. The Operational Plan is a commitment to meet the requirements of the Strategic Plan and is "owned" by the CEO.

What is strategic planning? Who participates in the planning process? How should a strategic planning session be designed for success?

Strategic Planning—What it entails

Strategic planning is the leadership function of

- Articulating why the organization exists
- Setting goals and objectives that will enable the organization to move towards fulfilling its reasons for existence
- Developing time-phased plans and identifying measures of success for meeting the goals and objectives
- Identifying who is responsible for meeting the goals and objectives
- Establishing a monitoring system

Let us look at each of the important parts of the definition in turn.

Strategic planning—the leadership function

Those who are charged with the leadership of the organization should be the ones attending the strategic planning session. This session is typically a one- or two-day event, often preceded by an extensive process of information gathering from members and stakeholders.

Many organizations will engage the services of an experienced external facilitator to coordinate the process and mediate the planning session. This method has the following benefits:

- As the facilitator takes on the coordinating role, this frees all of the participants (including the board chair and the CEO) to take an active part in the discussions.
- The facilitator can bring an independent viewpoint to the discussions.
- The facilitator can bring to the group experiences and solutions that have been successful in other organizations.

All volunteer directors (the policy-makers) should be present, together with senior staff of the organization (the implementers). Some organizations also like to invite a third group of "respected advisors."

Board members

If you cannot get at least 90% of the directors to come to the strategic planning session, then postpone the session! The strategic planning session is one of the most important activities your board will undertake during its term. If attendance is low, so will be the value of the outcome. To encourage attendance, as well as providing plenty of opportunity for the discussion of relevant issues, integrate a social component into the session that will allow time for the participants to informally meet and dialogue with one another.

Senior staff

Senior staff should not only help prepare for the meeting and attend the session but should also be encouraged to participate fully in the discussions and debates. After all, the senior staff will be developing the subsequent operational plans and budgets and then working on the implementation of the Strategic Plan on a day-to-day basis. In addition, their participation and input will add an essential, operational perspective to discussions.

However, the participation of senior staff should not eclipse the deliberations or decisions of the board. For instance, staff should not "vote" on any aspect of the plan, if indeed, things come to a vote. The Strategic Plan is "owned" by the volunteer board (on behalf of the members); it is the staff's responsibility to implement the plan to the best of their ability, regardless of their view of the plan.

Respected advisors

Who are they? These may be members who are neither board members nor staff, but who have a positive history of contributing to the work of the organization and whose views are respected by a broad spectrum of the membership. They may, for instance, include one or two past presidents, committee members, or perhaps a major sponsor or donor.

Articulating why the organization exists—the Mission Statement

This part of strategic planning is essentially about the development of the organization's Mission Statement. This key element in the planning process should be a clear, concise, and inspiring statement that declares what the not-for-profit organization is about, what it does, for whom, and where. The Mission Statement should be short enough that it can be readily reproduced on your website and letterhead, framed and displayed throughout your organization, or even printed on a T-shirt. It should be straightforward and simply worded. And most importantly, the Mission Statement should be the gauge against which every activity in the organization is measured.

Here are three examples of actual Mission Statements that meet those criteria:

> *The Canadian Cancer Society is a national, community-based organization of volunteers whose mission is the eradication of cancer and the enhancement of the quality of life of people living with cancer.*

The Mission of the College of Dental Hygienists of British Columbia is to protect the public by developing, advocating and regulating safe and ethical dental hygiene.

The Mission of the BC Bottle Depot Association is to advance the best interests of its members and promote sustainable recycling programs that support a healthy environment and benefit the public and our communities.

Make sure that you develop a Mission Statement that is "strategic" in nature and scope. It should focus on the long term, confirm the fundamental reason for your existence, and embrace all aspects of your operations.

Once the Mission Statement has been drafted and developed, it is important that all of the participants unanimously accept it. "Majority agreement," "reluctant acceptance," or "general consensus" is not good enough. This may seem an impossibly high approval threshold, but unless there is unanimous agreement on your mission, then the next steps of developing a Statement of Goals and Objectives (the road map of the organization) will be futile and irrelevant.

Establishing goals and objectives

When you have agreement on the Mission Statement for the organization, the next step is to develop some major goals and supporting objectives. Typically, four or five goals will be the most that any organization can hope to focus on and successfully work towards accomplishing over two, three, or four years. Once again, there must be unanimous agreement on the goals that are identified for the organization.

When you have decided upon your four or five goals, the strategic planners will then turn their attention to establishing specific objectives that support each of the goals. While this is the process followed at most strategic planning sessions, in some organizations this task of developing specific objectives will be delegated to staff or to committee(s).

Developing time-phased plans and identifying measures of success

Now you need to determine *timelines for completion* of the work (as well as for interim progress reports to the board) and identify measures of success in reaching goals and objectives. It may not be possible to determine in every case when each goal and objective can be accomplished, but as a minimum, the board should decide when it would receive progress reports on the status of the work. For example, the directors may decide that progress reports will be submitted at every board meeting.

In addition, at the planning session, the board must decide on how success will be measured. It is important to establish a *quantifiable measure of success*. For example, if one of the goals your directors want to achieve is to increase the number of members in the association, it is preferable to state the goal as:

- *Increase the number of association members during the next year by 15%*
rather than:
- *Increase the number of association members*

The difficulty with the second, non-quantified goal is that if there is only one more member next year, the goal has technically been met. However it is unlikely the directors would consider that a success.

Identifying who will be responsible for meeting goals and objectives

Don't let your planning session end without assigning the responsibility for the accomplishment of each goal and objective either to an individual or to a committee. By this means, you will establish an accountability framework that will increase the probability of successfully achieving your goals and objectives.

Establishing a monitoring system for the Strategic Plan

The last, and probably the most critical, element of the strategic planning process is to establish a monitoring mechanism to assess how the organization is progressing in meeting its objectives, its goals, and its mission. This monitoring function is where most organizations fail. We will provide more guidance on monitoring in Chapter 6.

EXHIBIT 2.1
Planning and monitoring
the Strategic Plan

Exhibit 2.1 illustrates how, in *planning*, the goals are developed to support the Mission Statement, and the objectives are developed to meet the goals. In *monitoring*, you start by looking at how the objectives are being met, then whether goals are being reached and how effectively these achieved goals successfully fulfill the mission of the organization.

About Vision and Values Statements

Do you need a Vision Statement and/or a Values Statement? If so, how would they relate to the Mission Statement?

A Vision Statement is a simple, concise picture of an ideal, desired future for the organization. What would complete success look like? For example, the vision of the Canadian Cancer Society is "Creating a world where no Canadian fears cancer." It is really the ultimate destination point at which there might even be no further need for that organization.

A Values Statement is a clear and concise statement of what values the organization, its employees, and its volunteers should observe as they work to fulfill its mission and achieve its vision. Typically, this statement emphasizes values such as integrity, respect, accountability, responsiveness, and teamwork.

While some consultants may advise you to develop all three statements—Mission, Vision, and Values—at your strategic planning session, I do not recommend this approach. With a few exceptions (e.g., a large national association with widely dispersed volunteers and staff), the added benefit of developing the Vision and Values Statements simply does not justify the time or cost of working on them.

Instead, you would serve your membership better by spending your valuable resources of time and money on developing a first-rate Mission Statement supported by appropriate goals and objectives.

The Operational Plan

The specific short-term activities of the organization that describes the tasks that are necessary in order to achieve its objectives are contained in the *Operational Plan*. Typically, the *Operational Plan* is developed by the CEO and staff, with input from the committees, after the Strategic Plan has been completed.

CHAPTER THREE

POLICY SETTING

POLICY SETTING

Supporting the strategic and operating plans of the organization is a broad range of policies that guide the organization and the decision-making of the board and the staff.

Role of the Board and CEO

What is the role of the board and the CEO in policy setting? This is one of the central topics of debate in the NPO sector. Peter Drucker writes:

> The conventional answer is that the board makes policy and the executive officer executes it. The trouble with this elegant answer is that no one knows (or ever has known) what policy is, let alone where the boundaries lie. [3]

A policy may be defined as

> a course or method of action that has been deliberately chosen and that guides or influences future decisions. [4]

---

[3] Drucker, 222.
[4] *Gage Canadian Dictionary* (Vancouver: Gage, 2000), 1136.

So when you develop policy at the board level, you are actively engaged in governing for the future of your organization. While there can be challenges in determining the respective roles of the board and the CEO[5] in policy setting, it is helpful to think of policies as being of two types— governing policies and administrative policies.

Governing policies

Governing policies include those policies related to

- Governing the volunteer organization; for example, board and committee organization, board director's code of conduct, and conflict of interest guidelines;
- Governing the membership; for example, membership requirements, categories of membership, membership responsibilities; and
- Governing the CEO; for example, code of conduct, conflict of interest guidelines.

The responsibility for *approving* governing policies rests with the board.

Administrative policies

Administrative policies are those that relate (a) to the administration of board-approved policies and programs, and (b) to the administration of the NPO office itself.

The responsibility for *approving* administrative policies rests with the CEO.

---

[5] In some organizations the chief executive officer may have the title of Executive Officer, Executive Director, President, or some other title. For brevity, we have referred throughout to this position as CEO.

Notice that we have so far referred only to the responsibility for policy approval (the board for governing policies; the CEO for administrative policies). But policies seldom come ready made—there is a creative phase, generally referred to as policy formulation. Here, there is typically some element of shared responsibility between the board and its CEO (and staff). The next sections of this chapter will explain the stages of policy formulation and how this cooperation can be achieved in large or small NPOs.

Six stages of policy formulation

There are six stages of policy formulation:

1. Identifying the need for a policy or policy review
2. Gathering information
3. Preparing options
4. Developing recommendations
5. Discussing options and recommendations
6. Deciding on policy (voting)

The two most important determinants as to how an NPO will deal with these six stages are the size of the staff organization and the size of the organization's budget. Generally, the smaller the staff size and budget, the more involved the board will be in doing the work for the six stages.

Formulating Governing Policies

We want to point out here a few differences in the approach to formulating governing policies in large-staff and small-staff organizations.

Formulating governing policies in large-staff organizations

In a large-staff organization (Exhibit 3.1), the identification of the need for a new policy or the review of an existing policy could be initiated by a director, by a staff member or, indeed, by any member of the NPO or the general public.

Suppose, for example, an issue has come up in Association X regarding the need for a code of ethics for members of the association, or in Association Y the matter of awarding honorary memberships in the association is unclear in existing policy. These would be governing policies.

EXHIBIT 3.1
Policy formulation:
Governing policies in large-staff NPOs

Stages of governing policy formulation	Board work	Staff work
Identifying need for policy or policy review	X	X
Gathering information		X
Preparing options		X
Developing recommendations		X
Discussing options and recommendations	X	X
Deciding on policy (voting)	X	

After the board has made a decision to review an existing policy or to formulate an entirely new one, the board would assign staff the tasks of
- Gathering information about the issue
- Preparing options for the board's review
- Developing recommendations for the board to consider

Both the board and the CEO would participate in the discussion of the options and recommendations, the CEO thus being available to provide background information to assist the board in coming to a decision.

However, when the board reaches the point of making a decision about which (if any) recommendation to approve, only board members would vote on the matter.

Formulating governing policies in small-staff organizations

How might the policy be written or modified in, say, an association with a small staff or even just a paid or volunteer administrator? Exhibit 3.2 shows one way the workload might be shared.

EXHIBIT 3.2
Policy formulation:
Governing policies in small-staff NPOs

Stages of governing policy formulation	Board work	Staff work
Identifying need for policy or policy review	X	X
Gathering information	X	X
Preparing options	X	X
Developing recommendations	X	X
Discussing options and recommendations	X	X
Deciding on policy (voting)	**X**	

In a small-staff organization, the identification of the need for a new policy or the review of an existing policy could be identified by a director, a staff member, a member of the NPO or the general public. In smaller associations, the chief executive officer may have the title of Executive Director, Administrator, or other title (we have referred to this position generically as CEO).

In such cases where staff and financial resources may not be available, once the board makes a decision to review or create the policy review, the remaining stages of formulation might be assigned to the CEO and/or to a group of volunteers—perhaps a task force specifically created to look into the policy issue (Chapter 4 has more on the concept of a task force).

Upon completion of its work, the CEO or task force would then submit the findings and recommendations to the board. Subsequent discussion of the options and recommendations would involve both the board and the CEO.

However, once again, when the board reaches the point of making a decision about which (if any) recommendation to approve, only the board members would vote on the matter.

Formulating Administrative Policies

The CEO has sole responsibility for developing the administrative policies of the organization. Depending on the staff size and budget, the CEO may call upon the assistance of volunteers in formulating these policies. In all cases, however, it is the CEO who holds the responsibility for implementing and controlling the administrative policies. As we did for governing policy formulation, we can consider the variants of this approach for large- and small-staff organizations.

Formulating administrative policies in large-staff organizations

Exhibit 3.3 shows a possible division of roles. In either situation, the need for a new administrative policy or the review of an existing one could be identified by a director, staff member, member of the NPO or the general public.

Suppose, for example, an issue has come up in Association X regarding the need for a policy on flexible working hours or work-sharing for staff, or in Association Y the frequency of making bank deposits is unclear in existing policy. These would be administrative policies.

EXHIBIT 3.3
Policy formulation:
Administrative Policies in large-staff NPOs

Stages of administrative policy formulation	Board work	Staff work
Identifying need for policy or policy review	X	X
Gathering information		X
Preparing options		X
Developing recommendations		X
Discussing options and recommendation		X
Deciding on policy		**X**

When the decision is made to undertake the policy review, the tasks of gathering information about the issue, preparing options for the CEO's review and developing recommendations for the CEO to consider would be assigned to the staff.

Discussion of the options and recommendations would involve both the CEO and other staff in the NPO. The CEO would then make a decision.

Formulating administrative policies in small-staff organizations

In a small-staff organization the assignment of work would be modified. Following the decision to review the policy, the CEO would proceed to develop a new or revised administrative policy. If there were insufficient staff or financial resources to undertake all of the necessary work, the CEO might assemble a group of volunteers to assist in the remaining stages. This group of volunteers would be called a CEO committee and would report to the CEO. Upon completion of its work, the committee would submit its findings and recommendations to the CEO, who would decide whether or not to accept and implement the recommendations. (Chapter 5 will provide more detail on the work of CEO committees.)

CHAPTER FOUR

BOARD COMMITTEES
AND
TASK FORCES

BOARD COMMITTEES
AND
TASK FORCES

Board committees and task forces should be appointed to address issues of governing policy. Effective committees make for good division of labour, provide opportunities for director and member participation, and often achieve much by cooperative teamwork. Committee experience can also be an excellent training opportunity for potential future members of your board.

Three Types of Board Committees

Three types of board committees are common in not-for-profit organizations. Each type is established by and reports to the full board.

The Executive Committee

Many not-for-profit organizations have an Executive Committee. This is often considered a "super committee" that is given the authority to act on behalf of the entire board between board meetings. It is important that the board, in its governing policies, defines the role of the Executive Committee with care and clarity because the board is legally responsible for the actions of all of the organization's committees, including the Executive Committee. The board will want to ensure that the Executive Committee does not act in a manner that would be inconsistent with the will of the majority of the board. Some organizations achieve this by limiting the Executive Committee's power such that the committee may not make any decisions without ratification by the full board.

Other board committees

The bylaws of the NPO will also normally give the board the authority to create other committees, if and when required.

A board committee, sometimes referred to as a board statutory committee, may thus be

- One required by the provincial/state/federal legislation governing the organization *or*
- One required by the organization's bylaws *or*
- One that is created by the board itself.

Board committees typically continue in existence on an ongoing basis from year to year, such as the Audit Committee or the Nominations Committee. The full board will often be assigned responsibility for approving the selection of the chair of a board committee and its members, although sometimes this responsibility is delegated to the board chair. Depending upon their level of activity, the committee may or may not provide reports for each board meeting.

Each year, the board should review and approve the terms of reference of the board committees to ensure that they are current and that, indeed, there is still a legitimate need for the committee.

Board task forces

The bylaws of the organization will also normally give the board the authority to create task forces if and when required. A task force is a "committee" established by and reporting to the board to assist the board by developing policy alternatives and recommendations for the board's consideration. When a task force is created, it is given a clearly defined task and a termination date (sometimes called a "sunset clause") for its activities.

For example, a board may establish a task force to examine and develop recommendations on a board policy dealing with membership criteria, membership discipline, ethics, or codes of conduct. Task forces should provide written reports for each board meeting.

Terms of Reference

When the board creates either a board committee or a board task force it should define, for each, the following terms:

- Purpose
- Chair and membership
- Responsibilities
- Meetings and time commitment
- Staff contact
- Budget

These *terms of reference* become a governance tool for the Board to monitor the performance of the committee or task force. An example of a board committee's terms of reference appears is provided in Exhibit 4.1.

ABOUT MANUALS

Board Governance Manual
This manual is designed for use by the volunteer board to help directors meet their responsibilities. It includes policies and procedures related to how the board operates, lists of committees and members, staff contacts, and key documents for reference.

Staff Policy and Procedures Manual
This manual is designed for use by the organization's staff. The CEO approves this material. The manual will vary considerably from one organization to another but generally contains operational instructions needed by the staff in order for them to meet their staff responsibilities.

EXHIBIT 4.1

Example of terms of reference for a board committee

> ## Ethics Committee
> Terms of Reference
> (Board Committee)

Purpose of the Ethics Committee

The committee will:

- Regulate the conduct of members in accordance with the bylaws of the Association.

Chair and Membership

The Ethics Committee consists of a chair and four members of the Association appointed by the Board of Directors.

Chair:	Kathy Gutierrez
Members:	Bill Jahutka
	Miles Standish
	Naomi Lim
	Sam Markus

Responsibilities

- Receive complaints from the public regarding the conduct of members.
- Investigate complaints and possible infractions.
- Resolve complaints with dispatch, fairness, and due regard to the trust granted the association.
- Advise the board, the members, and the public of its findings.

Meetings and Time Commitment

Committee meetings are held on the first Thursday of each month from 6 p.m. until 9 p.m. It is expected that, each month, members of the committee will be required to spend approximately six hours on committee work, over and above attending the monthly meetings.

Staff Contact

The staff contact for the committee is the Director of Member Services, who attends each committee meeting and takes the minutes.

Budget

The committee has a total budget of $ _____ including a meeting budget of $_____. No expenditures or commitments against the committee budget may be made without the authorization of the committee chair.

CHAPTER FIVE

IMPLEMENTING PLANS AND POLICIES

IMPLEMENTING PLANS
AND
POLICIES

Implementing the board's approved Strategic Plan and governing policies is the responsibility of the CEO and the staff of the organization.

The specific short-term activities of the organization that describe the tasks necessary to achieve its objectives are contained in the Operational Plan. As noted in Chapter 2, typically, the Operational Plan is developed by the CEO and staff, with input from the committees, after the Strategic Plan has been completed.

How Does the Organization Implement Plans and Policies?

A challenge exists in some organizations (especially small-staff organizations) where there may not be sufficient staff resources to develop and execute the implementation plan. The solution is to enlist the assistance of volunteers. Most small-staff organizations use this technique.

In such cases, it is important (and often forgotten) to distinguish between (a) a director's role in *policy development* as a member of the board and (b) a director's role in *implementing policies and plans*. In the latter role, the director is essentially acting in the capacity of "unpaid staff" and is accountable to the CEO for the work that has been assigned and accepted.

CEO Committees and Terms of Reference

A commonly used term for a committee charged with implementing a plan or a policy is *CEO committee*. The members of the committee are selected by the CEO, and the committee reports to the CEO. These committees deal with operational or management matters (not board governing policy), for example, the newsletter, fundraising, or conferences. Directors may serve on these committees but in this role, the directors report to the CEO. Reports on CEO committees may be included in the *CEO's Report* to the Board.

It is very important for the CEO to create terms of reference for each such committee, including the following:

- Purpose
- Chair and membership
- Responsibilities
- Meetings and time commitment
- Staff contact
- Committee budget

The terms of reference will make clear what is expected of the committee members and to whom they report. That will make it possible for the CEO to effectively monitor the work of the committee and be held accountable to the board.

An example of a CEO committee's terms of reference appears in Exhibit 5.1.

EXHIBIT 5.1
Example of terms of reference for a CEO committee

Newsletter Committee
Terms of Reference
(CEO Working Committee)

Purpose of the Newsletter Committee
The committee oversees the production of the association's quarterly newsletter.

Chair and Membership
The Newsletter Committee consists of a chair appointed by the CEO and at least two members of the association who have some knowledge or expertise in the publications field.

Chair:	Chris Lau
Members:	Michael Stadnyk
	Melanie Peterson

Responsibilities
- Maintain approved standards relating to all aspects of newsletter.
- Establish, maintain, and utilize the input from an editorial board.
- Ensure proper budget management for the newsletter.
- Solicit advertising for the newsletter.
- Organize and oversee the production of the newsletter.
- Report monthly to the CEO.

Meetings and Time Commitment
Committee meetings are held on the first Tuesday of each month from 6 p.m. to 9 p.m. It is expected that, each month, members of the committee will be required to spend approximately five hours on committee work, over and above attending the monthly meetings.

Staff Contact
The staff contact for the committee is the Director of Communications, who chairs committee meetings and takes the minutes.

Budget
The committee has a publication budget of $ _____ and a meeting budget of $ _____. No expenditures or commitments against that budget may be made without the authorization of the committee chair.

CHAPTER SIX

MONITORING

Monitoring

With so much activity going on in your organization, how can the board possibly keep up with everything? Well, it can't! The challenge for the board is to keep up with the most important functions in the organization and leave the rest to the paid staff. This board function is generally termed *monitoring*.

So, what should the board monitor?

Remember your dual role in leadership and stewardship (from Chapter 1). On behalf of the members and/or stakeholders of your organization, your dual role, in cooperation with other board members, is the following:

- Leadership: To decide where the organization should be going now and in the future.
- Stewardship: To ensure that as it moves forward, the organization's assets are as sound (or better) at the end of your term on the board as they were when you arrived (that means not only financial assets, but also reputation in the community and society).

To fulfill these roles you need to exercise leadership by monitoring organizational and people performance in relation to the mission and goals of your organization.

Monitoring Organizational Performance

As a board member with the responsibility to monitor the performance of the organization, you should have four key tools available to you:

- The CEO's Report
- Board committee and task force reports
- Financial reports
- External independent reviews

The first three items would be available for every board meeting. The fourth item would be presented as and when such reviews are undertaken.

All of these reports should be distributed in advance of the meeting to the board members so they would arrive ready to discuss them and if appropriate make decisions. These reports would not be read aloud at the meeting but those responsible for them (For example, the CEO or a task force chair) should always be at the meeting and be prepared to respond to questions about them.

The CEO's Report

This written report from the CEO should include:

- A summary of recent significant activities conducted by the organization's office staff, for example, a significant technology acquisition and/or implementation, or a major staff re-organization
- Updates on the work of the CEO committees
- A status report on the implementation of the Strategic Plan
- Other critical information of which the board should be aware

Board committee and task force reports

The chair of each board committee or task force should provide a written update on the work of their group, including a comparison to the approved workplan. In some cases, it may be prepared by a staff member but it is still the responsibility of the committee chair to approve it, present it to the board, and be accountable for it.

Financial reports

The written financial update from the CEO will include financial reports that are meaningful to board members. Financial documents that can only be interpreted and understood by professional accountants do not allow the board to meet its responsibilities. As a director, you have the right to demand financial information that you can comprehend. The report that you receive should include the board-approved budget and highlight variances from the budget.

External independent reviews

The board has the right at any time to engage an independent third party to review any management or policy area of the organization. The most common example of this is the hiring of an external auditor to review the financial statements of the organization. The independent reviewer would obtain instructions from the board, submit findings and, if required, recommendations to the board.

Monitoring People Performance

Standards of conduct and performance in an organization begin at the top—with the board. Even though directors and other volunteers are not generally paid for their service, they are still accountable to the board and membership for their conduct and performance. An effective "leadership" board will therefore develop a number of tools to assist in monitoring this area of responsibility. As you will see, these documents are more than just job descriptions. They establish codes of conduct for performance in the work of the organization, conflict of interest policies, and appraisal systems. Seven key documents are outlined below:

- Board Director's Code of Conduct[6]
- CEO's Code of Conduct[7]
- Conflict of Interest Policy for the Board and the CEO
- Conflict of Interest Policy for the Committees and Task Forces
- Board Performance Appraisal
- Individual Director Performance Appraisal
- CEO Performance Appraisal

Board Director's Code of Conduct

This document will outline the directors' expectations of one another and perhaps of the board as a whole. It goes beyond the job description and is more concerned with behaviour than specific duties. It will typically include clauses dealing with supporting board decisions, speaking on behalf of the organization, preparing for board meetings, conduct at board meetings, confidentiality, communication with staff, and ethical issues such as harassment.

CEO's Code of Conduct

This document will outline the board's expectations of the CEO. Again, it goes well beyond the job description and will include clauses dealing with the requirement to keep the board informed, the handling of member and stakeholder complaints, the treatment of staff, government filings, and communication with external parties. Any breaches of the Code would be reported to the board as part of the CEO's Report.

[6,7] These codes of conduct are to be distinguished from codes of conduct for members of associations of licensed professionals which govern ethical and other aspects of their professional practice.

Conflict of Interest Policy for the Board and the CEO

This document will outline the board's policy on conflict of interest. It will include clauses defining what a conflict of interest is, when and how a director or the CEO acknowledges that a conflict exists, rules related to confidentiality, access and use of insider information, giving and receiving gifts, and what corrective action is required by a director or a CEO who is in a conflict of interest situation.

Conflict of Interest Policy for Committees and Task Forces

This document will outline the board's policy on conflict of interest at the committee and task force level. It will include clauses defining what a conflict of interest is, when and how the committee member acknowledges that a conflict exists, rules related to confidentiality, access and use of insider information, and giving and receiving gifts. Corrective action at the committee level will normally be different from that at the board level. For example, unresolved conflict of interest issues or questions raised in a committee would be referred to the board for resolution.

Board Performance Appraisal

This document will provide a basis for the board to assess how it is performing, as a whole, in meeting its responsibilities. How well are board members informed about their role? How effectively does the board deal primarily with policy matters and avoid micro-managing the organization? How efficiently does the board monitor the implementation of the Strategic Plan? To what degree are board meetings an effective, efficient, and fair forum for discussion of issues? The board appraisals would be completed individually by the directors; collected, collated and reviewed by a board committee (for example, a Governance Committee); and recommendations would subsequently be provided to the board.

Individual Director Performance Appraisal

This document will provide a basis for the directors to undertake a self-evaluation of their individual performance on the board. Does the director understand the organization's mission, understand the role of the board and the CEO, adhere to the code of conduct and conflict of interest policies, regularly attend board meetings prepared to discuss, debate, and decide on the issues facing the organization? These self-appraisals would be completed individually by the directors; collected, collated, and reviewed by a board committee (for example, a Governance Committee); and its recommendations would subsequently be provided to the board.

CEO Performance Appraisal

Annually, the board should complete a written performance appraisal of the CEO. This will enable the board to identify areas where it is satisfied with the CEO's performance and areas where expectations are not being fully met. By identifying areas where improvement can be made, a plan for taking corrective action can be developed and implemented.

The entire board may want to participate in the appraisal process, or the board might delegate the task to a committee of the board. In some circumstances, the process might be expanded to include input from the CEO's staff and from stakeholders. This expanded appraisal process is often referred to as a *360° appraisal system*, because of its input from many directions.

CHAPTER SEVEN

GOVERNANCE MODELS

GOVERNANCE MODELS

G overnance can be defined as the manner in which structure, direction, resources, and accountability inter-relate and operate within an NPO. Different governance models define these relationships differently.

Given the diversity of not-for-profit organizations, each with its own unique history, culture and mission, it is unrealistic to expect that one single governance model would meet all of their different requirements. Membership size, financial resources, and the age and maturity of the organization can also influence the choice or evolution of the governance model.

Out of clutter, find simplicity.
From discord, find harmony.
In the middle of difficulty lies opportunity.

-Albert Einstein

Consciously or not, successful not-for-profit organizations generally adopt a model that adheres to some fundamental governance principles and concepts that have been developed over many decades.

Alternative Governance Models

In this chapter, we will describe the *Traditional Governance Model*, as well as two increasingly common alternatives. These alternatives are the *Complementary Governance Model* (based on the writings of Peter Drucker) and the *Carver* or *Policy Governance Model* (based on the writings of John Carver).

The *Traditional Model* was the most commonly used model until the late twentieth century. A recent survey by Association Management Consultants Inc. found that in British Columbia, Canada, 37% of the respondents reported that their organization followed the *Complementary Governance Model*, while 19% reported that their organization followed the *Policy Governance Model*.

Some 44% of organizations reported that they followed neither of these models. It may be safely assumed, however, that this group had combined elements of one or more of these models that in practice worked for them.

The Traditional Model

The *Traditional Model* of board governance, in its evolution through the last century has generally had these general characteristics:

1. The Board of Directors, headed by a Chair or President, actively participates in both the governance and management of the organization.

2. The board establishes all policies, including governing and administrative policies. The staff provides advice—largely restricted to administrative advice.

3. The board hires and fires a senior staff person (often termed

Executive Director, but may instead be called Administrator, Manager, Office Manager, or Executive Secretary). The board may also assume responsibility for hiring subordinate staff in the office.

4. The board approves the annual financial budget, which is prepared either by the board, the treasurer, a committee of the board, or the staff. The financial statements are prepared by the treasurer, a committee of the board, or the staff for review by the board. The board may set individual salaries, perhaps with recommendations from the Executive Director.

5. Board meetings deal with both governing policies and administrative policies and other matters. A Board Manual includes content relating to both, often including administrative office procedures.

6. All committees are board committees that are established by and report directly to the board.

7. There is usually an Executive Committee.

The Complementary Model of Board Governance

The *Complementary Model* of board governance is based upon these underlying principles:

1. The Board of Directors, headed by a Chair, is ultimately responsible for both the governance and the management of the organization. The board appoints and delegates management of the organization to a Chief Executive Officer (CEO).

2. The board develops all governing policies, such as codes of conduct, conflict of interest, and membership criteria.

3. The CEO develops all administrative policies required to run the organization.

4. The board approves the Strategic Plan of the organization and the annual financial budget.

5. Board meetings deal only with policy matters and performance monitoring.

6. There are three types of committees in the organization:
   - Board policy task forces
   - Board statutory committees
   - CEO committees

7. There are two policy manuals in the organization:
   - Board Governance Manual
   - Staff Policy and Procedures Manual

8. The board monitors organizational performance with the following tools:
   - The CEO's Report
   - Board committee and task force reports
   - Financial reports
   - External independent reviews

9. The board monitors people performance with tools such as these:
   - Codes of conduct
   - Conflict of interest policies
   - Performance appraisals

10. Board development and training is a priority, budgeted item.

> **Drucker on the complementary roles of board and staff**
>
> *Nonprofits waste uncounted hours debating who is superior and who is subordinate—board or the executive officer. The answer is they must be colleagues. Each has a different part, but together they share the play. Their tasks are complementary.*[8]

The Carver or Policy Governance® Model[9]

The key characteristics of the *Carver* or *Policy Governance Model* may be summarized as follows:

1. The Board of Directors works exclusively on policy development and on overseeing organizational performance by monitoring adherence to board policies.

2. All policies developed by the board fall into one of four categories:
    *   Ends policies, which direct the CEO to achieve certain results
    *   Executive limitations policies, which constrain the CEO to act within acceptable boundaries of prudence and ethics as articulated by the board
    *   Board/CEO policies, which define the ways in which the board and CEO will interact
    *   Board governance process policies, which define how the board as a whole, the board chair, and the committees (if any) will operate

3. The board can develop policies in any area it desires (administrative as well as governing), to any depth it desires; then subsidiary policy development at lower levels is delegated to the CEO.

---

[8] Drucker, 221.
[9] This section is based on information in Carver, *Boards That Make a Difference.*

4. The board appoints the chief executive officer (CEO) who is accountable to the board for achieving the "ends policies" of the board and has authority over the staff of the organization. The CEO must operate within the "executive limitations" policies of the board.

5. The Strategic Plan, long-term goals, and annual budget are created by and approved exclusively by the CEO, who can abandon or change any pre-existing versions.

6. The board monitors the CEO only against approved ends and executive limitations policies.

7. The board has three options for monitoring organizational performance:

   - *Internal Report*—The disclosure of compliance information to the board from the CEO.

   - *Direct Board Inspection*—The discovery of compliance information by a board member, a committee or the board as a whole. This is a board inspection of documents, activities, or circumstances directed by the board which allows a "prudent person" test of policy compliance.

   - *External Report*—The discovery of compliance information by an independent, external auditor, inspector, or judge who is selected by and reports directly to the board. Such reports must assess executive performance only against policies of the board, not those of the external party unless the board has previously indicated that party's opinion to be the standard.

8. Staff in the organization may appeal a decision, action, or policy of the CEO to the board if internal dispute resolution procedures have been exhausted, and the employee alleges either that board policy

has been violated to their detriment or that board policy does not adequately protect their lawful rights.

Which model is best for your organization?

Which model is best for your organization is, of course, a fundamental question for your board. I recommend that you study the alternatives carefully. Debate fully and deliberately the perceived benefits and drawbacks of each. Assess how the alternative models would "fit" with your organization's culture, future direction, stakeholders, and volunteers. Then make your decision.

Whichever governance model your organization adopts, it is supremely important that the board clearly articulates and documents the respective roles of the two halves of the governance and management partnership —the board and the CEO. It is useful to recall another statement by Peter Drucker:

> Thus each has to ask, What do I owe the other? not – as board and executive officers still tend to do – What does the other one owe me? The two have to work as one team of equals.[10]

It is likewise important that all of the leaders in the organization—the chair, executive, board members, and CEO have a clear and shared understanding of the selected model. That level of understanding can be heightened and reinforced by annual board orientation training sessions. Chapter 8 outlines the information that should be incorporated into this annual training.

---

[10] Drucker, 221.

Exhibit 7.1 COMPARISON OF GOVERNANCE MODELS

Function	Traditional		Complementary		Carver	
	Board role	Staff role	Board role	Staff role	Board role	Staff role
Strategic Planning	Approves	Provides limited input	Approves	Provides input	No role	Prepares
Budget	May prepare completely	Prepares for approval by the board	Approves	Prepares for approval by the board	No role	Prepares
Day-To-Day Operations	May have a role	Has a role	No role	Makes all management decisions	No role	Makes all management decisions
Review of Financial Statements	Reviews Balance Sheet and Income Statement	Prepares for review	Reviews periodic financial report that highlights variances from approved budget	Prepares the financial report that highlights variances, for board review	May have little or no role	Prepares for staff review
Financial Policies	Establishes all policies	Provides advice on policies	Sets some financial policies	Sets subsidiary policies	Sets some financial policies	Sets subsidiary policies
Personnel Policies	Establishes all policies	Provides advice on policies	No role	Exclusive role	Sets some personnel policies	Sets subsidiary policies
Administration Policies	Establishes all policies	Provides advice on policies	No role	Exclusive role	Sets some administration policies	Sets subsidiary policies
Hiring of Staff	Hires CEO and perhaps others	Has a role below CEO level	Hires only the CEO	Hires subordinate staff	Hires only the CEO	Hires subordinate staff
Staff Salaries	May set individual salaries	Recommends	Sets global budget and CEO salary	Sets subordinate salaries	Sets global budget and CEO salary	Sets subordinate salaries
Firing of Staff	May have a role	Has a role	No role except with regard to the CEO level	Exclusive role below the CEO level	No role except with regard to the CEO	Exclusive role below the CEO level
Staff Evaluations	CEO appraisal often verbal or not done at all. May evaluate non-CEO staff	Has a role in evaluating subordinates	Evaluates against CEO Code of Conduct and annual goals	Exclusive role below the CEO level	Evaluates CEO against Ends and Executive Limitations	Exclusive role below CEO level

72

Exhibit 7.1 COMPARISON OF GOVERNANCE MODELS						
	Traditional		**Complementary**		**Carver**	
Function	*Board role*	*Staff role*	*Board role*	*Staff role*	*Board role*	*Staff role*
Staff Grievances	May have a role	Has a role	No role	Exclusive role	Court of last appeal	Handles unless the staff grieves to the board
Title of Senior Staff Person		Varies widely but typically not President or CEO		CEO, sometimes also called Executive Director, Registrar, or President		Varies widely - CEO, Executive Director, Registrar, or President
Committees	All report to board	None report to Exec. Dir.	Some report to board	Some report to CEO	Some report to board	Some report to CEO
Board Manual	Lengthy- includes board policies and staff office procedures		Short- contains governing policies, mission, history, governance, description, committee terms of reference, and legal documents	Two separate documents: Board Policy Manual, and Staff Policy & Procedures Manual	Short - four types of policies: 1. Ends 2. Executive 3. Board/ Exec. Dir. 4. Board governance process	
Conflict of Interest Policy	Maybe		Yes		Maybe	
Volunteer Appraisal System	No		Yes		Maybe	
Executive Committee	Yes		Maybe. If yes, its role is clear and limited		No	
Board Meetings	Deal with policy and admin. matters		Shorter - deal only with policy matters and performance monitoring		Shorter - deal only with policy matters and performance monitoring	

CHAPTER EIGHT

BOARD TRAINING

Board Training

NPOs that do not have a structured program to train board members about their organization, and their roles and responsibilities within the organization, should not be surprised if these volunteers are unaware of these issues and are unsuccessful in meeting their responsibilities. It is as simple as that! Without proper training—such as at least a mandatory orientation session—the organization ends up with a group of well-meaning people doing the wrong things because they received no direction about the right things to do.

What to Include: Ten Key Topics

The volunteers on your board, and on your committees, need to have information related to ten key topics:

1. Their legal responsibilities as volunteer directors

What the law requires of NPO directors. In most jurisdictions this is spelled out in provincial/state or federal legislation.

2. Governance and management philosophy

The environment in which your NPO functions will likely be quite different from those in other NPOs in your community. For example, Chambers of Commerce do not have the same culture and expectations of volunteers that Rotary clubs do. So, it is important that your NPO offer training and guidance about how your group functions.

3. History of the organization

For directors and committee members to contribute to the NPO, it is important that they have a sense of the history of the organization, especially its past successes.

4. The organization's Strategic Plan

If the directors and committee members are going to be successful in helping move the NPO forward, it is important that they understand the organization's plans for the future. New directors may have their own views about the wisdom or the validity of the direction, but the starting point for any meaningful dialogue and debate is an understanding of the current Strategic Plan.

5. Board-approved policies

What policy decisions has your board already approved? This information has to be communicated to newly elected directors. This is particularly important in terms of the board's expectations for the conduct of the directors themselves. The policies for conflict of interest, codes of conduct, and performance appraisal should be provided as they apply to the board, CEO, and the directors themselves.

6. Legal documents of the NPO, including the constitution and bylaws

The general purposes of the organization and its general operating structure and procedures are described in the constitution and bylaws. This is important information for the directors to know.

7. Volunteer organization chart and contact list

Who's who in the organization and how to contact them for what type of information. Providing this information to the directors will prove very helpful, save them time, and make communicating easy.

8. Senior staff organization chart and contact list

Who's who in the senior staff organization.

9. Terms of reference of board committees and task forces

Much of what is accomplished by NPOs is done through board committees and task forces. Monitoring the activity of these groups is an important responsibility of the directors. Each director should have a clear understanding of all of the committees and task forces, and not just the one to which they personally belong.

10. Board minutes for the past year

Knowing what issues the board has been dealing with during the recent past will particularly help new directors ascend the learning curve at a faster pace.

Drucker on Training

What do these (volunteers) themselves demand? What makes them stay— and, of course, they can leave at any time. Their first and most important demand is that the non-profit have a clear mission, one that drives everything the organization does... The second thing this new breed requires, indeed demands, is training, training and more training.[11]

Designing an Orientation Program

The most successful way to improve the performance of your board and committee members is to periodically schedule a structured orientation program. A three-hour session, for example, facilitated by the senior staff or an outside professional, will provide an excellent forum and strong foundation for the volunteers' future performance. The orientation session should use the Board Policy Manual as the core curriculum.

The timing of the session is important. It will be of greatest value if it is held shortly after the new board takes office. If your circumstances will allow, it is also beneficial to have the chairs of committees attend. After a few opening remarks by the board chair and/or the CEO, the group can settle into an informal, but structured, session covering the important roles and responsibilities of your volunteers in your organization.

Remember that the volunteers' role in your organization may not be what the attendees have experienced in their volunteer work in other NPOs. As we noted earlier, business associations, such as the Chamber of Commerce, do not have the same culture and expectations of volunteers as charitable organizations. So, it is important that your organization offer training and guidance about how it functions.

---

[11] Drucker, 213

A successful orientation program for new and returning directors and committee chairs will result in a better-informed volunteer organization that will be ready to effectively govern your organization and move it forward in fulfilling its mission.

CHAPTER NINE

FINANCIAL
STEWARDSHIP

FINANCIAL STEWARDSHIP

In my experience, the boards of not-for-profit organizations truly appreciate the importance of prudence in managing the finances of their organization. They all treat their special status as an NPO as a "trust," and the directors are very diligent about monitoring the financial condition of the organization. This, without exception, has been my observation in working with over 350 NPOs across 18 years of consulting practice.

As a board, you want to be confident that the organization is demonstrating sound financial stewardship in three main areas:

- Cost containment
- Revenue maximization
- Internal financial controls

This chapter outlines a range of tactics used by NPOs in each area of stewardship. In many organizations, the CEO develops tactical proposals for the board to consider and approve (or otherwise). In other organizations, the CEO will actively pursue a tactic without seeking specific approval from the board because the tactic is clearly within the CEO's management area of responsibility.

Cost Containment

NPOs have successfully used a variety of methods to keep their costs as low as possible. Here are some ideas that may also be workable for your own organization:

- Sharing office space and, as a result, sharing capital assets such as photocopiers, fax machines, telephone systems, and receptionist services
- Contracting out professional services, such as bookkeeping, media relations, government relations, and website maintenance
- Partnering with other related NPOs for conference, trade shows, and speakers
- Conducting joint board orientation sessions with other boards
- Jointly producing common communications and public relations materials with other NPOs
- Conducting staff training in conjunction with other NPOs
- Consolidating administrative, human resource services, and webmaster services with other NPOs
- Arranging bulk purchase agreements in cooperation with other NPOs
- Routinely requesting trade discounts because of NPO status
- Routinely seeking competitive bids on significant product and service contracts
- Critically assessing the value of member and client programs and discontinuing those where cost exceeds value

Revenue Maximization

Two types of revenue streams flow into an NPO: dues revenue and non-dues revenue. For charitable organizations, dues revenues are generally less important, while donations (a non-dues revenue source) are paramount.

Dues revenues

The not-for-profit sector has undergone significant change in recent years. There are more NPOs than ever before, and in many fields they are competing more aggressively for members and membership dollars. In this environment, the key to keeping your dues revenues high is to maximize what I call the Membership Value Proposition.

The Membership Value Proposition (MVP)

The MVP may be stated as follows:

> *The value received (tangible and intangible) from belonging to the association must be equal to or greater than the cost of belonging to the association.*

Tangible benefits are usually easy to calculate. For example, if an association can arrange for cash discounts on products or services used by members and if these are greater in value than the dues paid by the member, then the member will see an economic gain in remaining in the association. NPOs have introduced a wide variety of member benefit programs with this proposition in mind. Some common ones are:

- VISA and MasterCard discounts for vendors
- Insurance premium discounts
- Training course/seminar registration fee discounts
- Group purchase discounts

It is important that the association select products or services that are of value to its members and negotiate a discount with the provider that will be made available exclusively to association members. Exclusivity is not always possible—but that should be your starting point in the negotiations with the supplier.

Intangible benefits present more of a challenge to cost, so here MVP is not as easily determined. What is the value to members of the camaraderie, the "networking" and business contacts, or sales leads arising from membership? How would one cost the value of status gained by belonging to the association? Often the best that an organization can do is to periodically survey its members of the organization for input about the *qualitative value* of the intangible member benefits. This information could be obtained in a number of ways including telephone, fax, email and mail surveys as well as face-to-face and focus group studies.

Making the Membership Value Proposition a reality at your NPO is more important now than at any time in the past. Given the economic constraints that businesses, professionals, and the general public have faced in recent years, many organizations' members have critically evaluated the worth of those memberships. On the basis of the value received for the cost paid, the MVP, they have made their decisions as to which organizations to support.

Non-dues revenues

Non-dues revenue generation has taken on increasing importance because of the challenges in generating dues revenue. Revenues of this type include:

- Advertising
- Sponsorship
- Trade shows
- Seminars and training programs
- Breakfast, luncheon, and dinner meetings
- Sports and other special events
- Insurance programs
- Credit card rebates
- Interest on investments
- Advisory services

The first role for the board before the organization embarks on any of these revenue-raising alternatives is to establish a policy that defines the NPO's revenue goals. For example, will some events be run on a cost recovery basis only or will all events be required to generate a profit—and if so, how much of a profit will be the goal? Will the board place restrictions on the type of investments that the NPO can make, thus affecting the revenue from interest? These are policy issues for the board to decide.

The board must also establish a monitoring system so that it will receive appropriate financial information on the results of all revenue-raising activities and thus be better prepared to take any corrective action that might be required.

Internal Financial Controls

The purpose of a system of internal financial controls is
- To ensure that the assets of the organization are safeguarded against waste, fraud and inefficiency
- To promote accuracy and reliability in accounting and operating data
- To encourage and measure compliance with approved policies
- To judge the efficiency of operations[12]

As part of the annual work of your NPO's auditors, they will review the systems of internal controls in your organization including areas such as these:
- Documentation
- Computer and internet security
- Segregation of duties
- Handling and recording of cash receipts
- Bank statement reviews and reconciliations

---

[12] Adapted from W. Meigs, E. Larsen, and R. Meigs, *Principles of Auditing*, 5th ed. Irwin, 1973.

The auditors will then submit a report that will include any concerns they may have about the internal systems in your organization. That report will often be in the form of a Management Letter addressed to the CEO and/or board. This represents a valuable, independent, third-party assessment of how things are working in your organization. As the Board of Directors, you should ensure that you receive a copy of the Management Letter and monitor the remedial action that is taken by the CEO to ensure that the auditor's concerns are addressed.

About Profit or Surplus

Nowhere is it written that NPOs are forbidden to make a profit (often called a "surplus" rather than "profit").

In fact, if you want your organization to survive and do great things, you had better plan to make a profit on every activity you organize: every luncheon, every dinner meeting, every golf tournament, every trade show, and every seminar—everything!

There are three important reasons to make a profit on virtually every activity you organize:

Confidence: You want the board to have confidence that there is sufficient revenue to support the programs that will lead to achievement of your mission. You don't want the fear of the lack of funds to divert the board's focus from this primary role.

Innovation: There will be times when your NPO will want to innovate, with a new program or project that you know will initially be a money-loser, but will subsequently be in the black. You will need the profits from other events to cover those initial losses that are sometimes the necessary cost of innovation.

Security: At some point, your NPO will fall on hard times (count on it!) and you will need the financial cushion from the profitable events to carry you through those lean times. Surplus can enhance your financial security.

How much is too much? How big a surplus or accumulated profit can you have? Check with your NPO's auditor or accountant, but generally your NPO will be fine as long as you don't have an amount greater than one year's operating expenses in the bank. So, for example, if it costs your NPO $500,000 a year to cover all of your operating expenses, typically, you can build up an accumulated surplus of $500,000 without being concerned about any tax implications.

CHAPTER TEN

MEETINGS:
TEN SIMPLE RULES

MEETINGS:
TEN SIMPLE RULES

Governance is about providing leadership. Good leaders know how to run good meetings! This applies equally whether you are the chair of the board, or the chair of a committee or task force.

Meetings are a great opportunity not only for the chair but also the participating members to demonstrate leadership and stewardship as they make the decisions on behalf of the membership and thus fulfill their governance responsibilities.

A meeting is a centuries-old forum for debating, discussing, identifying problems, strategizing, solving problems, developing and monitoring action plans, and moving an organization in the right direction. Meetings should be welcomed as venues to achieve in some measure the mission, goals, and objectives of the organization.

The intent of this chapter is to offer guidance for better meetings, including ten simple rules for more effective use of this medium of communication and decision making. We will avoid delving into the finer points of Robert's Rules of Order, but will provide a handy chart of the generally accepted way for the business of a meeting to be conducted—how to amend a motion, object to a procedure and so on (please see Exhibit 10.1).

Board Meetings: Roles of the Chair, Directors, and Others

Let us begin by defining the role of the board chair and (other) directors.

Board chair

The board chair (or a delegated meeting chair) performs many functions in ensuring that board and membership meetings are productive. They include the following:

- Preparing the agenda
- Confirming that the meeting is properly called and constituted
- Calling the meeting to order
- Calling for approval of the agenda and any changes
- Conducting the meeting according to the agenda
- Preserving order at the meeting
- Deciding on points of order and procedural issues
- Deciding who properly has the right to speak
- Putting motions to the vote
- Declaring the results of the vote
- Ensuring that the minutes are prepared and distributed
- Setting the time and location of the next meeting

Directors

Directors at a board meeting also have responsibilities to fulfill. These include:

- Arriving at the meeting on time
- Being prepared for the meeting by having read the pre-circulated materials
- Being respectful of their colleagues and their views
- Debating issues and not personalities
- Knowing how to make and amend motions
- Attending the meeting until it is adjourned

Other participants

It may be necessary for other people to attend board meetings: they may include the CEO, senior staff, other members, and consultants. The chair makes the decision to invite them and calls on them to speak to issues or answer questions if and when appropriate. These invitees must understand that they are under the control of the chair. As a general rule, they would not join in discussions but only provide information, though this practice may vary in some organizations. They would not, however, make motions or vote.

Other Types of Meetings

In addition to board meetings, most organizations have committees or task forces that hold their own separate meetings, with their own chair and committee membership. The duties of the chair and participants are similar to those outlined above for the board chair and directors.

A particularly important type of meeting is that of the general membership such as the Annual General Meeting (AGM) or a special-purpose meeting of the general membership, known as an Extraordinary General Meeting. The chair and participants in such meetings essentially have similar responsibilities as outlined for board meetings.

Ten Simple Rules for Success

A meeting can be the most effective way of unleashing the creative energy, the imagination, and the hands-on ability of volunteers and staff. But if poorly planned and conducted, a meeting can be the most ineffective, time-wasting, frustrating experience ever inflicted upon volunteers and staff. Usually, the problem is not the meeting—the problem is the organizer and the participants!

Here are ten simple rules that will help ensure the success of board meetings. Most of them also apply to other meetings such as committees and task forces.

1. Prepare and pre-circulate the meeting agenda and attachments.

Make sure that you or the staff distributes the agenda and materials that are to be considered at the meeting, well prior to the meeting. This material should include the reports from the committee chairs and the CEO.

2. On the agenda, indicate the meeting start time and end time.

In today's environment, time is at a premium. The agenda should indicate not only when the meeting will start but also when it will end. This will allow the participants to plan their time schedule for before and after the meeting. In addition, it will give the participants a target to shoot for in terms of completing their work.

3. Start your meetings on time.

One of the biggest failings of volunteer chairs is that they do not start the meeting at the appointed hour. This sends the wrong message to two groups:

- *Those who showed up on time.* The message is: "Thank you for arriving on time, but it really doesn't matter because I never start on time."
- *Those who showed up late.* The message to them is: "You didn't miss anything because I never start on time."

You should assure participants that you value their time and cooperation—start every one of your meetings promptly at the time shown on the agenda.

4. Do not recap for latecomers.

Another failing of many volunteer chairs is that they believe that have a duty to latecomers to recap what has already been dealt with. This, too, sends wrong messages to:

- Those who showed up on time: "Not only will you have to participate in the meeting as we work through the agenda, but you will have to sit through it all a second time for the benefit of the latecomers."

- Those who showed up late: "Don't bother being on time because I'll always go over what you missed when you do finally arrive."

As an effective chair, you should reward those who arrive on time and encourage those who consistently arrive late to show respect for their colleagues.

5. Use a "consent agenda."

A *consent agenda* is a section of the main agenda that can address routine items that will likely require no discussion (Exhibit 10.2) It permits the group to make one motion to "accept, adopt, and receive" a number of items with a single vote.

It works like this: Prior to voting on the consent agenda, the chair will ask whether anyone would like any item removed from the list. If an item is removed from this list, it is simply transferred to an agreed position in the main agenda. A director does not have to provide any rationale for requesting this move. The remaining items are then dealt with by a single motion to "accept, adopt, and receive the items in the consent agenda."

6. Keep a speakers list.

While each agenda item is being dealt with, the chair should keep a list of the names of the people who have indicated (in order) that they wish to speak about the item. This enables the chair to follow the list so that each person who has requested time to speak will be called upon in turn. By following this simple practice, the chair will help bring fairness and order to the discussion. The group may also decide to adhere to the practice that each person will be allowed to speak to the item under discussion only once, until everyone who wishes to speak has done so.

7. Allow only one speaker at a time.

The chair should encourage orderly discussion by not allowing cross-talk or side discussions while a speaker has the floor.

8. End meetings on time or earlier.

If you are efficient and have everyone's cooperation, you will be able to work through your meeting agenda in record time while still allowing adequate time for full discussion and debate. As a result, you will be recognized as a chair who exercises leadership at meetings and provides a sense of satisfaction to the participants.

9. Have "action minutes."

A set of well-constructed minutes of one meeting form a solid foundation for the next. As chair, you should ensure that the minutes of the meeting identify what tasks are to be undertaken, by whom, and by what date. If the three Ws (What, Who, and When) are clearly shown in the minutes, you are more likely to achieve your goals.

10. At the first meeting you chair, give people your plan.

As a new chair, when you call your first meeting to order, take a few moments to explain to your colleagues how you intend to chair the group's meetings. Let them know about the practices (such as the "rules" recommended here) that you will follow at meetings. Explain the purpose—to make effective use of their valuable time. Ask for their cooperation so that you can work together to accomplish the board's mission, goals, and objectives.

Meeting Management Grid and Sample Agenda

On the following pages you will find a grid summarizing the different types of motions that may be used at a meeting (Exhibit 10.1). This is a simple version adapted from Robert's Rules of Order which should make the formalities easier to follow for any chair or participant. Following the grid is a sample meeting agenda format (Exhibit 10.2)

Exhibit 10.1 MEETING MANAGEMENT - ALL YOU REALLY NEED TO KNOW

In Order To	May the Person Speaking Be Interrupted?	You say	Must There Be a Seconder?	Is the Motion Debatable?	Is the Motion Amendable	What Vote Is Required?
Adjourn the Meeting	NO	I move that we adjourn	YES	NO	NO	Majority
Recess the Meeting	NO	I move that we recess until...	YES	NO	YES	Majority
Complain about noise, etc.	YES	Point of privilege	NO	NO	NO	None (chair decides)
Suspend consideration of something	NO	I move we table it	YES	NO	NO	Majority
End debate	NO	Call the question	YES	YES	YES	Two-thirds
Postpone consideration of something	NO	I move we postpone this matter until...	YES	YES	YES.	Two-thirds
Have something studied further	NO	I move we refer this matter to a committee	YES	YES	YES	Majority
Amend a motion	NO	I move that this motion be amended by...	YES	YES	YES	Majority
Introduce business (a main or primary motion)	NO	I move that...	YES	YES	YES	Majority
Object to procedure or to a personal affront	YES	Point of order	NO	NO	NO	None (chair decides)
Request information	YES (if urgent)	Point of information	NO	NO	NO	NO

In Order To	May the Person Speaking Be Interrupted?	You say	Must There Be a Seconder?	Is the Motion Debatable?	Is the Motion Amendable	What Vote Is Required?
Object to considering of some improper matter	YES	I object to consideration of this question	NO	NO	NO	Two-thirds
Take up a matter previously tabled	NO	I move we take from the table...	YES	NO	NO	Majority
Vote on a ruling by the chair	YES	I appeal the chair's decision	YES	YES	NO	Majority

EXHIBIT 10.2 MEETING AGENDA FORMAT USING A "CONSENT AGENDA"

BOARD OF DIRECTORS
NOTICE OF MEETING
AND
AGENDA

DATE:　　　　Monday, April 26, 20XX
TIME:　　　　3:30 pm to 5:30 pm
LOCATION:　Boardroom, Association Office
　　　　　　　503 W. Fort St., York City

AGENDA

1. **Call meeting to order and Chair's remarks**　　　3:30 pm

2. **Acceptance of agenda**　　　3:35 pm

3. **Consent agenda:**　　　3:40 pm
   3.1 Adoption of the minutes of the last meeting
   3.2 CEO's Report
   3.3 Financial Report for the first quarter of year
   3.4 Annual federal filing

4. **Business arising (not elsewhere on the agenda)**　　　3:50 pm
   4.1 AGM – Information only: Venue update (Previous Minutes Item 6.1 - Don Cohen)
   4.2 Public licensing - Decision on legal action (PMI 6.4-Allen Brown)

5. **Committee reports**　　　4:20 pm
   5.1 Governance Cte. - Decision on Board orientation session (Dave Pitout)
   5.2 Audit Cte. - Information only: Update (Sara Allibhai)
   5.3 Members' Code of Conduct Task Force - Decision on New Members' Code of Conduct (Lynn Nazbul)

6. **Other Business:**　　　5:20 pm
   6.1 Annual Filing - Information needed from the Directors (Jeff van Dijk)

7. **Date, time, location of next meeting and adjournment**　　　5:30 pm

Moving Forward – Together

> *What is the use of living, if it be not to strive for noble causes and to make this muddled world a better place for those who will live in it after we are gone?*
>
> - Winston Churchill

There are tens of thousands of not-for-profit and charitable organizations doing important work in our society. Whether they are classified as charities, trade associations, professional associations, special interest associations, professional colleges or some other category, they all have one common characteristic. They rely heavily on volunteers to help them accomplish their goals. They rely on people to come forward who will, without expectation of monetary gain, contribute innumerable hours of time and effort to accomplish something bigger, something better, something together.

It is as though thousands of grains of sand have come together to have more force and more impact than any one of them could have alone.

Too often these grains of sand, these volunteers, behave as though a strong wind had descended—buffeting them here, there, and everywhere. They lack focus, fly about in multiple directions, bumping into one another, expending energy but accomplishing little that is useful.

The purpose of this book—to create a short, self-contained guide for NPO success —arose from my experience working with volunteer organizations to help their boards exercise effective leadership and sound stewardship. I hope that you have found in it some practical ways to contribute to your own board so that together you can make this muddled world a better place in which to live.

Tom Abbott
Vancouver, Canada

ISBN 141207595-5